| surprises | laughter | tears | purpose |
| lessons | joy | hardships | distance |

JOURNEY

jour·ney/ˈjərnē/

noun

An act of traveling from one place to another.

| fear | triumph | hope | anticipation |
| frustration | peaks | valleys | celebrations |

Testimonials

Powerful, honest, real, motivating and heart-wrenching. These are the words I would use to best describe 'My Baby Journey.' Karen takes you on an impact-filled journey of her own fertility struggles and leaves no stone left unturned. She shares it all--the good, the bad and the ugly! No matter if you are single without children or already have a whole clan of your own, this journal will leave you inspired and encouraged to walk through your own journey in a healthy manner

--Kiaundra Jackson, LMFT, Licensed Therapist, TV Personality, Speaker and Author

Karen masterfully synthesizes the authenticity of her personal journey with the depth of her psychological expertise and grace. Women long for a space to share the necessary and uncomfortable parts of the human experience. This guided journal accomplishes just that. What a remarkable endeavor it is to celebrate the gift of motherhood while helping others still on the journey of trying to conceive.

--Myesha Chaney, Writer & Speaker

Karen Balumbu-Bennett, LCSW, PMH-C

MY BABY
JOURNEY

A Guided Journal to Support You Through the Peaks
and Valleys of Trying to Conceive

To maintain the anonymity of the individuals involved, some names have been changed. This book does not replace the advice of a mental health or medical professional. This book contains my memories, from my perspective, and I have tried to represent events as faithfully as possible.

This Journey Belongs To:

_____

(me)

Table of Content

Prologue

Thank you for allowing me to join you on your baby journey. This is a very special and complex time, and I am honored that you have decided to use this journal as a guide. The road to parenthood isn't always how it is portrayed in the movies: linear and easy breezy. For some, the road is filled with numerous speed bumps, potholes, dips, and turns. For others, the road is filled with days of anticipated excitement, that are then met with gut wrenching disappointment.

I hope this journal can guide you with processing the many thoughts and feelings that accompany the challenges of conceiving. When my husband and I were in the thick of trying to get pregnant, we both experienced a roller coaster of emotions. We were so caught up in our conflicting emotions that we did not always process our feelings or share our grief with others. We internalized our feelings, which caused problems for our individual emotional stability and our relationship. Even as a licensed clinical social worker and therapist, I found it challenging to manage my own emotions, despite the education and training I've acquired throughout the years. Though I have provided supportive counseling to hundreds of individuals, when I was experiencing one of my toughest challenges, I did not fully recognize the amount of external support that I needed.

This guided journal is intended to help you process the ups and downs of the family planning journey. There are no limits to how you use this journal. If you are on this journey with a partner, you and your partner can use the same journal, although I strongly advise that each individual has their own. You can go in chapter order, or jump around. You can also come back and add more to a particular section. Included in the back of the journal are appendices and resources to support you. Use the feelings chart, the list of coping skills, and the other appendices provided to assist in your processing. This journal belongs to YOU, and you have the freedom to personalize how you will use it... I simply provide a guide by sharing some of my personal experience and professional expertise to help you along your journey.

I hope you feel validated, encouraged, and supported. I hope this journal is a safe place for you to process and vent. For those who are completing this journal as a couple, I hope this journal serves as a "mediator" - a way to assist you in understanding your partner's viewpoint. In all, my hope is that this journal gives you a necessary outlet that I didn't have when I was on my journey. And of course, my hope is that whatever the outcome of your journey, that you can look back at your experience and find comfort in the choices you have made.

Well Wishes,

~Karen

Before You Begin

Terms You Should Know

Cognitive distortions – Ways of thinking that are negatively biased, habitual, and often false (e.g., blaming yourself for everything wrong, expecting the worst, etc.).

Coping skills – Clinical "tools" consisting of behaviors or activities that strengthen a person's ability to cope with stressful or negative situations.

Defense mechanism - A mental process (e.g., repression, denial, or projection) usually unconsciously activated to avoid anxiety or conflict.

Infertility - The inability to become pregnant after a year of trying (or after 6 months of effort if the woman is 35 years or older). If a woman can get pregnant but keeps having miscarriages or stillbirths, that's also called infertility.
NOTE: Birth workers are choosing to use the phrase Fertility Challenges instead of infertility.

Intrauterine Insemination (IUI) - A fertility treatment that involves placing sperm inside a woman's uterus to facilitate fertilization. The goal of IUI is to increase the number of sperm that reach the fallopian tubes and subsequently increase the chance of fertilization.

In Vitro Fertilization (IVF) - The process of fertilization by extracting eggs, retrieving a sperm sample, and then manually

4

combining an egg and sperm in a laboratory dish. The embryo(s) is then transferred to the uterus.

Mindfulness - A mental state achieved by focusing one's awareness on the present moment, while calmly acknowledging and accepting one's feelings, thoughts, and bodily sensations.

Negative self-talk - A mix of negative conscious and subconscious thoughts and dialogue that we have with ourselves.

Perinatal Mood and Anxiety Disorders (PMADs) - A newer, more comprehensive term than Postpartum Depression (PPD), that recognizes that the perinatal time can induce not only depression, but also other mood and anxiety disorders (e.g., bipolar, post-traumatic stress disorder [PTSD], psychosis, OCD, anxiety).

Physical Indicators (of) Stress – The physiological response to stress. Physical symptoms of stress include: headaches, muscle tension, low energy, digestive issues/stomach pains, rapid heartbeat, lowered immune system, low libido, clenched chaw, increased perspiration, insomnia or hypersomnia.

Positive self-talk – A mix of positive conscious and unconscious thoughts and dialogue that we have with ourselves.

Self-Care - The practice of taking an intentional and active role in protecting one's own well-being and happiness, in particular during periods of stress. Self-care is a lifestyle practice.

Identify Your Support Systems

A key first step on your journey is to identify your support systems. Use the area below to identify colleagues, neighbors, friends, and family who you can rely on for various forms of support. Who are the people in your life that can cover that work project, distract you from worrying, or support with household chores? Even if you are on this journey with a partner, it is wise to consider others to help broaden and strengthen your support network. We don't always realize this, but often, the people in our lives support us in different ways. For instance, some are great listeners, others are always down to go out and have a good time, some give great advice, while others will accompany you on a nice nature walk. You may even have a person in your life that may stop by and bring you a warm homemade meal when you are down and out. If you think really hard, I am sure you will realize that in some instances, you have certain people in your life that already play these supportive roles, and perhaps, you will be able to identify one person who has many of these qualities. In any case, I strongly encourage you to identify people in your life that can step up and help you during your baby journey.

If you are the type of person that has a difficult time asking and/or accepting help, this is NOT the time to refuse support. The baby journey (i.e., before, during, after), is a time to receive. Be open to allow those that care about you to step in when needed. Community care goes a long way!

MY SUPPORT SYSTEM

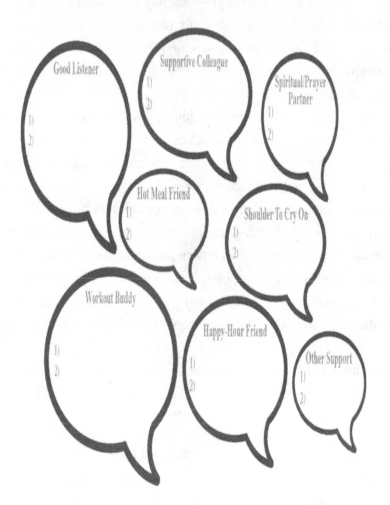

Part 1: So You've Been Trying To Conceive

When my husband and I decided to become intentional about having a baby, we never imagined months and years would pass, and we would still be trying. We never imagined that we would use ovulation tracking apps, ovulation tracker strips, or herbs. We never imagined that he would get his sperm count checked, and that I would have numerous medical tests conducted. We never imagined that we would have to even consider alternative ways of conceiving or having children. This realization was a huge blow to our ego and expectations. We had to take the time to grieve and mourn the idea of how we were going to become parents and what that process would look like. For the first time, we had to consider, what if this doesn't happen for us? That was a reality that we both struggled to process.

It is important to acknowledge the rollercoaster of emotions, from excitement to disappointment that is attached to this journey. There are times that your period is a couple of days late, or your breasts are a bit more tender to the touch than usual. Other times you are certain you engaged in intercourse at the right time and will for sure be pregnant, only to be disappointed by either your period starting or a negative pregnancy test. When these events or situations occur, they trigger thoughts, oftentimes unconsciously, and from those thoughts, emotions develop. Typically, most of us don't process our thoughts, and we may jump to having strong emotions or strong behaviors.

Many of us do not realize that our thoughts are powerful. Changing the way we think ultimately changes our mood and behavior. When we have negative thoughts, it is important for us to recognize them, and consider challenging them. If we can challenge our negative thoughts, there is a possibility that we can lift our mood.

The Cognitive Wheel, as pictured below, illustrates the notion that our thoughts, feelings, and behavior are all interconnected: Situation/Event → Thoughts → Feelings → Behavior → Physiological response. Remember the more you spend time processing your thoughts, the better you will become at identifying negative thoughts and challenging them.

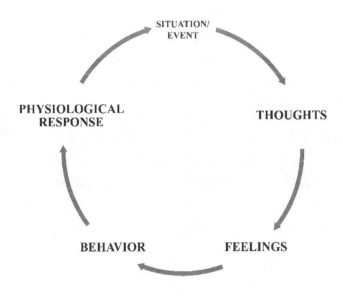

Here is an example of how the same event/situation can produce different behavior outcomes as a result of challenging negative thoughts.

Thought Log

EXAMPLE:	Event/Situation	Thoughts	Feelings	Behavior	Physiological response (*Not always present or easily identified)
	*My Period was 3 days late, but started today.				
My automatic processing	*My Period was 3 days late, but started today.	This is stupid; I'm never going to get pregnant.	Sad, disappointed, hopeless, frustrated	Cry, isolate for a few days, overeat	Stress headache
Alternative processing	*My Period was 3 days late, but started today.	This is disappointing, but I'll try again next month.	Frustrated, hopeful, slightly sad	Somewhat withdrawn for a few hours	None

Challenging your thoughts to allow yourself to consider a more positive or neutral thought doesn't always mean that your mood will do a 180-degree turn; however, what it will almost certainly do is positively shift your mood and potentially change your behavior and outlook.

11

In this section, take the time to journal about your current thoughts and feelings. Feel free to draw a chart similar to the one above. Our thoughts directly impact our feelings, so take some time to really explore the various thoughts flooding your mind. Allow yourself to sit with your thoughts. How are these thoughts serving you? Journal about any negative thoughts and then challenge your negative thoughts by writing alternative ways to think about the situation.

Carve out time to
reflect, process,
and reconnect
with YOU!

Part 2: Is This Ever Going To Happen For Me/Us?

I want to normalize that you may be grieving what you expected your baby journey would be. Grief is not solely about a physical loss of a loved one, but it is also a loss of a dream, loss of an experience, and loss of an expectation. Grief is not linear; it comes and goes like waves.

After almost two years of trying to conceive, I began feeling really hopeless. I never imagined that having a baby would be so difficult. Now, I wasn't naïve. I personally knew people who had various challenges with either getting pregnant or staying pregnant, but I never envisioned that I would fall into that category. I began strongly doubting that it would ever happen. My unconscious negative thoughts evolved into me actually speaking negatively about our chances of conceiving. I found myself struggling with challenging my negative thoughts, which made room for me to become more skeptical and less optimistic. At this point, I transitioned my research from supportive aides that help with conceiving, and began to do more research on fertility challenges as a whole, more specifically, the length of time it typically takes people to conceive.

I know that "*Dr. Google*" is not always recommended; however, for my processing, I needed to learn more about the realities of conceiving. While researching and reading articles, understanding that the roughly 10% of women who struggle with conceiving and/or staying pregnant amounts to 6 million plus women, made me feel less alone and validated. I also learned that approximately one in eight couples experience fertility challenges. And though I read these numbers a dozen times before, at that moment, it clicked... fertility challenges were not uncommon and there is a community of people out there who unfortunately are going through similar hardships. Interestingly, although we were approaching three years of actively trying, I felt a bit encouraged to keep pushing through. I read stories about how people became pregnant after years of trying, and at the moment, I felt a bit hopeful that I could have the same outcome. During this time of researching, I realized that for many, trying to have a baby does take time, even though people often only share the joyous end result. Though researching and reading success stories provided a small glimmer of hope for me at that particular time, researching and reading on-line stories is not recommended for everyone. It is important that you monitor how your mood is impacted by what you are consuming.

Please remember that you are not alone in this journey. Unfortunately there is stigma associated with people having fertility challenges, and many feel isolated and forced to keep it a secret for fear of being judged or having to hear unsolicited comments and/or advice. Allow yourself to grieve the loss of your expected and hoped for baby journey. You may experience some or all of the stages of grief (reference Appendix D). It is important for you to show yourself compassion and to always allow yourself to feel your feelings.

In addition to challenging your negative thinking, also known as cognitive distortions, another tool that can elevate your mood when feeling down and/or doubtful, is to regularly practice positive self-talk. Positive self-talk includes the intentional act of affirming yourself. Please keep in mind that for some people, affirmations are only impactful if they are realistic and fact based. For instance, telling yourself *"I am a conqueror"* or *" I am bigger than this situation"*, may not be helpful if you are feeling extremely low. I recommend you create a list of times in your life where you overcame difficult situations or times where you exceeded your own expectations. That action will help you link meaning and proof to your affirmations.

The chart below provides more information about positive self-talk and cognitive distortions/negative thinking.

Positive Self-Talk & Negative Thinking

Positive Self-Talk	Common Cognitive Distortions /Negative Thinking
The act of intentionally shifting your internal & external dialogue to be more positive focused. Cognitive Distortions develop overtime and affect our unconscious and automatic self-talk. It's important to become aware of them so that you can begin to challenge them.	Personalizing - Blaming yourself for everything. Catastrophizing - expecting the worst, and rarely allowing reason or logic to change your mind. Polarizing - Seeing the world in black and white, or good and bad. Not allowing for a middle ground to categorize or process life events. Magnifying - having a laser light focus on negative aspects of a situation, while ignoring any or all of the positives.

In this next exercise, process any grief you may be experiencing regarding your expected family planning experience. (Reference Appendix E: Stages of Grief). Allow yourself to freely and honestly journal about any fears and concerns that you have. In Part I, we learned about the power of our thoughts. Now focus on acknowledging not only your thoughts, but also, your negative self-talk. Begin to challenge your negative self-talk and try to speak positivity. Remember, try to keep affirmations realistic and fact based.

Also, use this section to begin to journal about your next steps in this journey. Journal about what actions (research, medical, supplements, tracking, etc.) that you are willing to take, and those you are not ready to incorporate. Explore the reasons behind your choices as you journal. Consider referencing the resource section of this journal as needed.

DATE   /   /

Carve out time to
reflect, process,
and reconnect
with YOU!

Part 3: Considering Taking a Break

F or some of us on this journey, there comes a time where we decide to take a break from trying to conceive. We find ourselves consumed with everything baby, and it's only right that we step back and regroup. I remember the first time my husband and I took a break... oh yeah, we took a break more than once. The first time, I decided to take the break; the second time, it was my husband who insisted we take a break. Regardless of who makes the decision to hit the pause button on baby making, it's important that you both are honest and communicate. For those who are on this journey as an individual, it's important that you are honest with yourself about your thoughts and feelings surrounding taking a break.

When I decided to take the first break, I felt like I was drowning. I found myself being irritable, and easily frustrated. Typically, I am a fun go-with-the-flow type of person, and I found that the recurring cycles of upsets were slowly altering my personality. I realized that I did not like how frequently my mood was despondent, or how negative I was becoming. It took some time for me to recognize these changes, but once I did, I was certain that the best thing for me was to minimize the pressure I was carrying. The monthly task of trying to conceive was wearing on me. Therefore, taking a break was long overdue.

Researchers have debated for years whether high amounts of stress can cause infertility. The verdict may still be out, but we all can agree that fertility challenges can surely cause stress. In addition, studies have found that people who are struggling to conceive secretly struggle with depression, anxiety, and loss of control. Research has also found that the degree of depression found within infertility patients is similar to those patients struggling with cancer. Think about how heavy that is. And now think about how you, me, and others have been trying to carry this burden alone. It is A LOT to carry! I know for me, the stress of trying to conceive directly affected my physical being. For instance, I would get migraines, lose my appetite, and my muscles would constantly tighten. It became important for me to use coping skills such as deep breathing and mindfulness to help me manage the stress. Whether stress directly impacts fertility or not, allowing yourself to take time away from baby making, can help you regulate emotionally. Restoring a balanced lifestyle, if nothing else, is beneficial for your mental stability and all around Wellness.

Before you begin to journal, use the next page to identify your physical indicators of stress. Think about how your body reacts to stress. For instance, do you feel knots in your stomach, do you get sweaty palms or underarms, tightness in your chest, or perhaps restless feet? Begin to create a list of coping skills that you can use to manage stress in the moment (Reference Appendix C: Coping Skills).

STRESS INDICATOR

Draw lines to the different areas of your body where you physically feel stress. Then use the chart below
to identify two coping skills that you can use to help manage symptoms.

When you are upset, where do you feel it?

Stress Indication	Coping Skill #1	Coping Skill #2
Ex: Headache	Rest	Hydrate

In this section, journal about your reasons for taking a break. Explore how long you would like for this break to last. What is something you can let go of in order to invite more balance into your life? How will you intentionally fill your time during this break? Write down some activities that you can do during this time. Continue to identify and process negative thoughts.

DATE   /   /

MY BABY JOURNEY

Part 4: Finding Me/Us Again

During this "break time" or "refocusing time" it is important to continue to be intentional about spending time with yourself and to remember all the things you enjoy doing. I remember on my 6th year wedding anniversary, I didn't want to celebrate publicly. I didn't want to post on social media that we were celebrating six years of marriage because I dreaded the comments and questions that would end up under the post... the "when are you two having babies", "can't wait until the two of you have a little one", or one of the worst, "**what are you waiting for**?". Family, friends, colleagues, associates, social media friends, and everyone in between could easily make a statement or ask a question that would send me down an emotional spiral that I was desperately trying to avoid. But in my efforts to avoid being bombarded with painful questions, I was neglecting to celebrate our union. My husband, Wayne, reminded me of that. He was hurt that I was "blah" about our anniversary. He hated that I wasn't excited to celebrate six years of being married. Although I understood his position, I had a really hard time shaking my baby woes. I finally pulled myself up, with his help, and enjoyed the weekend we planned. We decided to take our first train ride as a couple, down the coast from Los Angeles to San Diego and spent the weekend near the beach. It was exactly what I needed, and it was what we needed. I laughed, danced, and didn't worry about what others may ask or say. That was the beginning of finding me again and getting back to us.

Following our trip, I realized that it was no longer enough for me to only use coping skills when necessary; I needed to be more intentional about incorporating self-care into my lifestyle. There is a slight difference between coping skills and self-care. I like to think of coping skills as intervention and self-care as prevention. Coping skills are the tools you tap into, in the moment, to manage stress, anxiety, frustrations, etc. While self-care activities are practiced as a routine to help promote a more balanced life. Keep in mind that some coping skills can evolve into self-care activities if you practice them regularly and include them in your lifestyle. For example, regular meditation and mindfulness can allow you to feel more focused and centered daily (self-care), but can also help manage and reduce frustrations when practiced during stressful moments (coping skill).

What self-care looked like for me was increasing my workouts from 2 days to 4 days a week, regularly getting better sleep, praying and/or practicing mindfulness every morning, and taking more breaks throughout my workday. This was a great start and really helped me focus on myself, and ultimately on us as a couple.

In this next section, take some time to journal about the overwhelming process of trying to conceive (TTC). Couples should take this opportunity to journal separately. Be honest with yourself. Is your relationship struggling? Are your external relationships struggling? What aspects of your "pre TTC" life do you miss most? How has your sex life or intimacy been impacted? What are some things you can do to regain some balance? Identify some self-care activities that you can immediately incorporate (Reference Appendix D). Is there anything your partner can do to help with the "finding us" process? Identify your thoughts and self-talk that may need to be challenged if necessary.

SELF-CARE LOG

Identify self-care activities that you can begin to incorporate into your lifestyle. Reference Appendix D for ideas.

Self-Care Activity	Frequency	Start Date
Ex:Yoga	Bi-weekly	Sunday

Carve out time to
reflect, process,
and reconnect
with YOU!

Part 5: The Reason I/We Haven't Been Able To Conceive Has Been Identified

A t some point in this journey, all parties involved (e.g., you or you and your partner), will most likely decide to get tested by a medical professional. Getting a series of medical tests will allow for a diagnosis and possible answer(s) to the reason you haven't been able to conceive. Your diagnosis will fall into one of three categories: male factor, female factor, or unexplained. Some people dread this part of the journey, because of the stigma associated with infertility. Society has attached our "manhood" and "womanhood" to our ability to procreate. Men feel like "less of a man" and some women believe they are a failure or are less desirable, if they are the identified partner having fertility challenges. If you have been feeling stuck and tired of being in the unknown, it's best to take the next step to discover what that problem may be.

When our doctor finally informed us that the reason we were struggling to conceive was primarily male factor, it crushed Wayne. He wasn't crossing his fingers behind his back hoping that the test results would determine it was a female factor problem, but deep down, he also didn't want to feel that he were the cause of why we weren't pregnant. He felt as if he failed me and failed us.

Below is an unedited excerpt from an essay Wayne wrote for a chance to be awarded a fertility scholarship, this is shared with his permission.

I'll start this off by being completely transparent in sharing that this is not a subject I am completely comfortable talking, or even writing about. I often push this subject to the back of my mind because, well, it makes me feel inadequate. As a man, and a husband, I want to be able to provide for my family in every way possible, (Spiritually, Emotionally, Financially, and Physically). I can admit that I am still learning the path of being a good steward in regards to many of these areas, but the area I had the most faith in, the area that I believed was a God given right, turned out to be the same area that has been my biggest disappointment.

For the last 4 ½ years of my marriage, my wife and I have attempted to become pregnant and have our first child. It was something that we decided together, and at the beginning it was all about having fun, and enjoying one another. As a couple of years went by, it became increasingly apparent that this was a little harder than what we had initially expected. I'll share here that month after month I would say to myself, "This is it, this is the month we get pregnant". I did my best to keep a strong face, and faithful stance for my wife, but with every month that passed it became harder to continue being that rock, as it hadn't happened. And, I knew deep down that I was probably the reason.

Going to the Dr.'s and finding out that I had a low sperm count was very hard to hear. Witnessing my wife's mood change every time she received her period, the tears, and that lack of motivation to even try anymore has been a burden I've had to carry alone. I didn't want my wife to know I had any doubt or that I had become angry because I felt less than. So, I continued to have a positive outlook for both our sake. It was something I felt I could do for us in the midst of finding out that I wouldn't be able to give my wife her greatest desire on my own.

When I read Wayne's essay for the first time, I was overcome with emotion. I guess I always knew that he was probably being hard on himself, but I didn't realize to what degree. Most of the time, I actually thought he wasn't as worried about our challenges with conceiving. I assumed that since his biological clock wasn't necessarily "ticking away", that he didn't feel the same level of urgency or disappointment that I felt. He didn't appear sad or upset, which I realized after reading his essay, was a defense mechanism. I often didn't know how to support him. I definitely didn't blame him. However, I was so deep underwater in my own feelings that I didn't always know how to be there for him. So what I did instead was jump into fixing mode. I researched and purchased herbs he could take. I researched and provided advice about limiting alcohol consumption, altering his diet, and even changing the type of underwear he should wear. I even connected both of us to an acupuncturist who specializes in fertility. However, I didn't always lend a listening ear, I didn't ask him how he would like to be supported, and eventually we both became so focused on solving the problem that we stopped processing our feelings. Don't do what we did! Try to find the balance between processing your feelings and finding a solution. Balance doesn't always mean equal, but instead that you are giving the proper amount of attention and effort to different areas of your life as needed.

In this section, journal about your thoughts and feelings regarding your test results and diagnosis. Have you been tested yet (why or why not)? What are your thoughts about being tested? How are these thoughts serving you? Is the reason you haven't conceived identified to be female factor, male factor, or unexplained? Were you surprised at the results? What are the medical professionals suggesting? How can you challenge the negative thoughts that may be flooding your mind? How can you redefine your identity in a way that is not tied to procreation?

DATE / /

Carve out time to
reflect, process,
and reconnect
with YOU!

Part 6: How Do I Support My Partner?

T his journey can seem exceptionally isolating. It is important for all the individuals involved to find their own support system. For those who are on this journey with a partner, let me tell you, it is absolutely necessary for you to also support one another.

We all deal with stressors differently. In part 3, we began the discussion of stress and how stress can impact our bodies. Here are more negative behaviors associated with stress; overeating/ undereating, negative thinking, angry outbursts, substance use, and depression. Some people even experience stress related somatic symptoms such as headaches, changes in sex drive, acne, gastrointestinal issues, insomnia or hypersomnia. Be mindful of how this process is not only impacting you, but also how it may be affecting your partner. Being proactive in recognizing and managing your stress is key; and the more aware you are in recognizing how this process is impacting your partner, the better you will be at supporting them. Support will look different for each person. Be mindful that there are limitations to how much support you can provide or receive from your partner, friends, and family. For some of us on this journey, seeking support in the form of professional help (i.e., therapy) may be extremely beneficial.

As I mentioned in the last chapter, you have to be intentional about supporting one another. You have to check in with each other and spend time talking about other topics aside from your baby journey. It's especially important for the partner that wasn't identified as having fertility issues, to reaffirm the identified partner.

The two of you are in this together, and should listen to each other and make decisions as a team. This journey is extremely emotional, and at times, partners are on different pages because feelings and pride get in the way. Vow to make a conscious effort to refrain from making emotional impulsive decisions and vow to defeat pride if it rears its ugly head.

In this next section journal about the following: When was the last time you were 100 percent honest about your feelings regarding your Trying To Conceive (TTC) journey? If applicable, why don't you feel comfortable being honest? When was the last time you asked your partner about their honest feelings? Could you handle their honest feelings? What are your thoughts about the identified reason that you haven't conceived? How do you plan on supporting your partner and affirming your partner? What are some negative thoughts that you are currently battling with and how can you change them from negative to neutral or positive?

Carve out time to
reflect, process,
and reconnect
with YOU!

Part 7: Creating Healthy Boundaries And Respecting My Feelings

One of the hardest things to do during my baby journey was to honor myself and set new boundaries. Being constantly bombarded with questions such as, "When do you plan on having a baby?," "What are you two waiting for?", or statements such as "Don't wait too long", could easily ruin my day. I found myself wavering from loosely explaining that not being pregnant wasn't by choice, to flat out lying with replies such as, "I know huh, we better get to it". I didn't always know how to respond. There were times where I tried the honesty route, but then I was met with more intrusive questions, rude statements, or unrealistic, unrelated, and unsolicited advice. For example, I remember once I shared with an older woman at church something to the extent; "It hasn't happened yet... we've been trying for a while, it's a bit discouraging, but just keep us in your prayers". Her response was something similar to, "just don't think about it, that's how I got pregnant... just don't wait too long, you're not getting any younger". Huh? How is that your reply? I was so annoyed, probably almost cursed right there in church! I realized that some people are not asking me questions because they really care about my response, but perhaps because they like to hear themselves talk and give advice. And others simply don't know how to respond or how to support in an effective way.

I knew that I couldn't avoid the irritating questions or rude statements forever unless I completely isolated myself. That wasn't what I wanted to do, nor is it a healthy choice. So, I made a decision to take a break from attending baby showers and kid birthday parties. I found those events to be too overwhelming for me. At birthday parties, being in the company of parents as they shared parenting stories and helped their children with juice boxes, became an uncomfortable setting. I was no longer interested in hearing them share stories about their "little angels". Baby Showers were even worse. Something about a baby shower made every person in attendance feel the need to ask others who did not have children, the million dollar question: "So are you (two) next?" At that point, I resolved that if I willingly subjected myself to that level of annoyance again, that I would punch myself in the face. Okay, maybe not punch, but you get the point. I couldn't continue to engage in settings where I knew 100% without a doubt that at least 10 people would believe they were asking a profound question regarding my conception plans.

My decision to skip birthday parties and baby showers didn't go over too well with everyone. One friend, in particular, even called me out on it. She noticed that I missed a couple of her children's birthday parties, and honestly, she probably noticed that I was distant in general. I finally explained to her that attending a kid's birthday party isn't that fun for an unintentionally kidless adult. I would typically attend to be supportive and it is nice to see the children in your life laugh and have fun. However, something that was already a challenge with a busy weekend to-do list, became even less of a priority considering the emotions and unwanted questions that accompanied me to these parties. I was glad that my friend asked me about my distance. I wasn't sure if she could completely understand my plight, but it seemed as though she was able to become more empathetic.

50

I also realized that shutting people out or failing to be forthcoming in explaining why I'm behaving differently, leaves people to their own assumptions. This interaction helped me decide to be more assertive with friends and family. It wasn't always as easy to assert myself with associates or colleagues, but at least I was getting better at telling friends and families my limits and boundaries. I realized with some people in my life, I had to squarely say, "I Don't Want You To Ask Me Questions About This Topic", because subtlety did not work. I realized the more honest and direct I was, the less I had to deal with unwanted questions and/or statements, at least within my closest networks.

In this section, journal about the following: What do healthy boundaries look like to you? What questions/statements have been the most irritating? When the questions/statements are coming from strangers and/or associates, how do you plan on handling it? When the questions/statements come from friends and family, how do you plan on addressing them? Can you benefit from being more assertive? Are you being honest with your loved ones about how their words impact you? Are you beginning to internalize the negative thoughts of others, if so, how can you challenge those negative thoughts? Are there any boundaries you need to set? If so, with whom? Take some time to sit with and process your overall feelings.

Carve out time to
reflect, process,
and reconnect
with YOU!

Part 8: I/We Decided To Try Alternative Methods (IUI/IVF)

After three years of trying to conceive, months of falsely thinking I was pregnant, days of crying myself to sleep and crying during my drive to work, I finally made the decision to try Intrauterine Insemination (IUI). Wayne wasn't completely on board with IUI. He didn't feel the same urgency I did at the time; however, he went along with the plan to try IUI. The clinic we attended at the time recommended IUI as one of our initial interventions. The doctors appeared to be most concerned with Wayne's test results; however, they often enthusiastically reminded us that "it only takes one sperm".

Three months and 3 failed IUI cycles later, I felt completely defeated. This was the lowest part of my journey. During this time, I had a clique of girlfriends; we called ourselves, "The Real Housewives of So Cal", a spin-off of the popular reality show. None of us were actually housewives, but we thought it was a cute name. Two of us desperately wanted to get pregnant and we were both struggling to conceive. The other two were open to having children one day, but were not as eager as myself and my friend Tish. To all of our surprise, one by one, each friend got pregnant all within the same year, and I was convinced that I too was going to have a baby alongside them. How could I not? It seemed too perfect that we would all make this life transition at the same time.

But with each failed IUI cycle, I realized that I wasn't going to conceive. I put my big girl pants on and attended each baby shower, genuinely happy for each friend, and simultaneously absolutely devastated for myself. I felt extremely lonely! In a matter of six months, my childless wives club was no longer. I felt alone, robbed, and I didn't understand why God was keeping me from going on this journey with my girlfriends. I was so grief stricken that I couldn't continue to put myself through the disappointment of failed IUI's. I told Wayne that I needed a break from trying to conceive… that break went on to last for a year and a half.

During my break, I remember having a brief discussion with one of my spiritual leaders. This particular individual is someone who can simply look you in your eyes, and immediately know that you have been going through a tough time. The type of person you occasionally avoid because you can't pretend that everything is "okay" around them. One day after church service, she walked up to me, and simply asked, "how are you doing?" I replied, "I'm well, how are you?" She slightly tilted her head, didn't answer my question, and just stared at me, as if she knew "I'm well" was as rehearsed as a ballet recital. I immediately knew that I wasn't getting out of this. I wasn't about to lie. I was still standing in the middle of church, so I just decided to give her an update on my baby journey. She knew that Wayne and I were having some challenges with conceiving, but was not aware about our medical tests and failed IUI's. She was happy to hear that we tried IUI and was glad to know that we were open to considering In-vitro Fertilization (IVF) in the future. She shared about past encounters with Christian women who were conflicted about moving forward with IVF. And though I wasn't having those conflicting views, it was nice to hear how she supported some of the women and how religion can play an important role within this journey. It was comforting being vulnerable with her; she validated my feelings, which made me even more confident in considering IVF as a future option.

When I was ready to resume our baby journey, I decided to try another fertility clinic. It never sat well with me that although Wayne's test results were the results that doctors were most concerned with, they still believed the problem was possibly female factor. Also, during the tail end of my break, Wayne and I began seeing an acupuncturist who specializes in fertility challenges. After viewing our test results, she believed that IUI was a waste of our time, money, and an ineffective form of treatment considering Wayne's motility and mobility count were low at the time. Her recommendation was that we give her six months to a year to help Wayne improve his numbers before moving forward with IVF. However, since we were already on the tail end of our break, I was over the idea of waiting any longer, so I decided to move forward with IVF in conjunction with acupuncture. After researching other reputable clinics in the area and scheduling consultations, I found our clinic.

Luckily for us, I became pregnant on the first IVF cycle. The process was not fun at all. The monthly payment on the medical loan we took out cost more than my car note. The extra hormones in my body made pregnancy even more challenging for me. The self-administered shots were a headache and a buzz kill, but at the end of the day, it was all a part of my baby journey. My special, turbulent, emotional, crazy, beautiful journey. It is a journey that has become a part of my story; and now that I am in a better space emotionally, I try to share my experience with others so that they know that they are not alone even though they may feel lonely.

In this section of the journal, if applicable, write about how you will support your partner during this process, and how you believe you would like to be supported during this process (i.e., emotionally, attending appointments, support with shots, etc.). Take some time to process the pros and cons if you are considering having multiples. Which IUI/IVF cycle are you on? What are your thoughts? How are you feeling (physically/emotionally)? If you have tried IUI/IVF and it did not work immediately, process how you are feeling. If applicable, how many IUI/IVF cycles will you do before deciding to take a "break"? Remember, it's important to have a flexible plan surrounding taking a break. If you believe going through IVF treatments conflict with your religious views, take time to process your thoughts/feelings/beliefs here. Remember to continue to challenge any negative thoughts you may be experiencing.

DATE / /

MY BABY JOURNEY

Part 9: I'm/We're Pregnant!

When I found out that I was pregnant, I was ecstatic. I was emotional and overwhelmed with joy. That feeling lasted for about four hours while I celebrated with my husband and called my mom, sisters, and best friend. But after the celebration died down, another emotion hit me… fear. I was terrified. Terrified that something would go wrong. Terrified that I wouldn't make it to term. Terrified that my results were a false positive. Whatever negative thought you could think of, I had it. Some of these fears lingered for the majority of my pregnancy.

I found myself hesitant to share the news with our extended friends and family. I surely did not want to post the infamous "I'm pregnant post" on social media. I then found myself upset that I was, in some ways, robbing myself of that pure excitement that first time moms get to experience. You know, the type of innocent excitement that isn't ushered in with the trauma of fertility challenges. I knew that my mood wasn't what I envisioned or what others would expect it to be, but it was really difficult for me to shake it. This caused problems between Wayne and myself. He didn't feel my same fear; but he understood my unwavering decision to wait to announce after the first trimester once I explained to him how the chances of miscarriage significantly reduce after that pregnancy mile marker. However, once we made it to the second trimester and he was eager to share the news with everyone, I still wasn't quite ready. He wanted to respect my wishes, but it was upsetting to him that he couldn't get the support that he desired because we weren't sharing the news.

I shared my feelings with one of my friends who also struggled with conceiving. My friend, Tish, part of the "housewives crew" and one of the three friends who conceived all around the same time, got pregnant naturally after trying for 5 years and being told by fertility doctors that she only had a 5% chance of conceiving without assistance. Tish was able to validate my feelings of fear, especially my fear of being scared to share the news. She too experienced let down after let down, and she feared that if something went wrong, she would have to experience disappointment with more people than she would like. Conversely, Tish also shared that when she and her husband did decide to share the news with more friends and family, they realized that they now have more people praying for them, sending positive thoughts, and supporting them. Talking to her was so helpful. She normalized my feelings and gave me some things to consider. The choice to share or not to share was still up to Wayne and I, but I walked away from that talk feeling less afraid.

On a crucial side note, one thing that Wayne and I did not do was really enjoy each other before our baby was born. If you can take a babymoon, do it! If you can do dinners, picnics, staycations or movie dates, do it! Enjoy your solo time, and your time together. Because your journey has been filled with lots of twists and turns, it's especially important to make sure that you reconnect with yourself and your partner prior to your baby's arrival.

How do you anticipate you will feel once you receive the

news about your pregnancy? How will you try to enjoy your time prior to your baby's highly anticipated arrival? How can you make sure that you are being intentional about honoring your self-care? Although you planned for this baby, the reality of parenthood hits some harder than others. Take some time to journal about any thoughts, fears or concerns you may have. For those that are on this journey with a partner, how can you support each other through this pregnancy? How can you solicit help from others (i.e., support system) during your pregnancy? Are you able to have a babymoon? If so, where and when? Discuss your birthing plan (i.e., doula, midwives, hospital, home birth, etc.). Process whether you are experiencing fear surrounding announcing your pregnancy. When will you announce your pregnancy? What are some negative thoughts that you are experiencing? What are some alternative neutral/positive thoughts that can combat the negative thoughts? It's important to feel your feelings. Don't deny your feelings whether they are fear, discomfort, or happiness. They are your feelings, they are valid, and it is important for you to acknowledge, to feel, and to process all of them.

Also, if you believe that you are experiencing severe emotional symptoms, you may be suffering from Perinatal Mood or Anxiety Disorders (PMADs) commonly referred to as Postpartum Depression (PTSD), if so, reach out to your OBGYN or a Mental Health professional as soon as possible.

Carve out time to
reflect, process,
and reconnect
with YOU!

65

Part 10: Waiting For A Positive Pregnancy Test/Experiencing Miscarriages

Every person's road to parenthood looks different. The degree of highs and lows vary from person to person. Time and time again, I found myself in a state of confusion and disbelief and was simply lost in the reality that I had yet to conceive. Each failed cycle of IUI left me feeling hopeless, withdrawn, isolated, and emotionally drained. I remember after my third failed IUI attempt, I started to have some internal dialogue asking myself if I would be okay if I never carried a baby. I started to explore how much I really desired parenthood and if I could find fulfillment in other ways. I processed if being a foster parent, "the cool childless aunt", or if adopting would be my journey to parenthood. In retrospect, trying to plan my future in my time of hopelessness wasn't the best idea. I was too deep in my feelings and not in the best mindset to clearly plan an alternate course to something that was so important to me.

During the time when I was struggling to process my failed IUI attempts, I was introduced to a woman named Laurel. I met Laurel during one of my much needed girls' night happy hours, where another friend invited her. Laurel openly shared about the agony of experiencing not one but four miscarriages. She shared how people would obnoxiously ask her questions such as, "what are you waiting for?" and "why haven't you guys had any kids yet?" She shared about how family members would make statements such as, "don't wait too long", and "girl, you should've had three kids by now". Hearing Laurel share, I was heartbroken for her.

At one point while she was sharing, there was a Charlie

Brown moment, where she was talking but I checked out and was trying to manage my rapid thoughts. I sat there comparing our disappointments, determining what was worse; my journey of not conceiving, or her journey of conceiving but not going to full-term. Finally, I realized that it wasn't about whose journey was "worse", "harder", or more traumatic. There was no competition. What mattered was that I was in a safe space speaking to other women about challenges that most people keep locked up in the depths of their internal diary. I realized that I found a community to cry with, to encourage me, to validate me, to challenge me, and most importantly to just be there for me.

This journey can be long, difficult, and emotional. Be kind to yourself and return to Part III (Considering Taking A Break) as needed. Take some time to process your emotions. If you are on this journey with a partner, it's important that you and your partner process together, examine all options, and talk about every step. My hope is that you take care of yourself and use this journal as a guide to help you process your thoughts and feelings along the way. Sending positive vibes your way... stay encouraged.

Use this time to freely journal about your current thoughts and feelings (Remember: Situation → Thoughts → Feelings → Behavior). Share your raw, unfiltered emotions. Reference the feelings chart (Appendix A) if you are having a difficult time identifying your true feelings. How many days have you been feeling this way? If you are on this journey with a partner, have you checked in with them (why or why not)? Write about the grief you are experiencing. What exactly are you grieving (e.g., a dream, an expectation, parenthood, etc.)? What stage of grief are you in? (Appendix E: Stages of Grief). How can you show yourself some compassion? What self-care practices are you intentionally employing? Explore what you need at the moment, review your social support list, and identify at least 3 people who you can lean on.

Carve out time to
reflect, process,
and reconnect
with YOU!

Conclusion

Thank you for allowing me to be a part of your journey. Everyone's path to parenthood is unique. My hope is that this guided journal allows you to better understand, honor, process and express your feelings. I also hope that, for those of you who are on this journey as a partnership, you feel more connected and able to share your thoughts, feelings and concerns with one another. We've all been sold the idea that conceiving is easy and pregnancy is a breeze, and though that is the case for some, that is not everyone's reality. Struggling with conceiving can leave us feeling isolated, anxious, lonely, sad, angry, hopeless, envious, and/or confused. There are a number of emotions that hover over us while in this season of life. Please remember that you won't be in this space forever, but while in it, try your best to show yourself compassion and take care of yourself.

I hope that you feel proud that you committed to using this journal as a processing tool. It is definitely easier to choose to ignore or even project your feelings. Doing inner work is hard and you've done just that! You have searched your heart to reveal your true feelings. Remember, this is a journal that you can revisit. You have extra writing pages that I encourage you to use if you need to return to a chapter and further explore your inner thoughts. Through pain there is an opportunity for growth, and the development of purpose. My hope for you is that by the end of this journal you feel more equipped to manage your emotions and express yourself. I want you to feel more empowered to assert yourself to your friends and family that continue to ask you about your journey, or worse, to those who make insensitive statements. I also hope that you feel more prepared to plan how you will address situations relating to your baby journey in the future. I hope that you've developed more support systems and that you have a more secure plan on how to manage the rollercoaster of emotions. I hope that you know that these hardships do not make you "less than" nor do they define you. You are brave, you are dedicated, and you are resilient. Continue to seek support as needed and prioritize your overall wellness. Again, thank you for allowing me into a small yet significant portion of your world, for trusting me, for allowing me to support you, and unknowingly supporting me in growing in my purpose.

Peace and Love,

~Karen

Appendices

FEELINGS LIST

HAPPY	ENCOURAGED
SAD	EXHAUSTED
HOPEFUL	DETERMINED
DISAPPOINTED	RENEWED
FRUSTRATED	MOURNFUL
EMBARRASSED	DISCOURAGED
INDIFFERENT/ BLAH	ANNOYED
MAD	SUPPORTED
NERVOUS	OPTIMISTIC
SCARED	CONTENT
LONELY	GRATEFUL
LOVED	FORGOTTEN
SURPRISED	JUDGED
CONFUSED	CURSED
UNDERSTOOD	BLESSED
EMPOWERED	CRUSHED
STRESSED	BETRAYED
DEFEATED	JEALOUS
GUILTY	EXCLUDED
PREPARED	AGITATED
	IRRITABLE

FEELINGS THERMOMETER

As humans we experience a number of feelings. The feelings thermometer is used to help us
"Check In" with our emotions. It is a way for us to recognize our mood elevation,
to then examine ourselves and identify our feelings, which then allows us
to employ the proper coping skills in order to regulate.

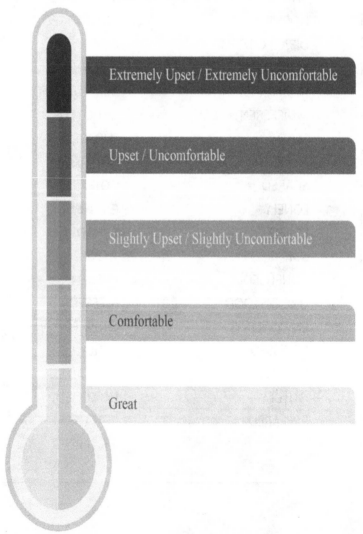

COPING SKILLS

Coping skills are tools or activities used to regulate emotions while in the moment. You will find that certain coping skills are more helpful at different times. Coping skills fall into various categories, including: self-soothing, mindfulness, distraction, emotional awareness, and social support.

Key: Think intervention over prevention.

Activities:	
BREATH	Take 3 slow deep breaths (repeat as needed)
COUNT	Start at 10 and slowly count down to 1 (repeat as needed)
ENGAGE YOUR SENSES	Name 5 things you see, 4 things you feel, 3 things you hear, 2 things you smell, 1 thing you taste
OUTDOORS	Step outside and feel the sunshine and/or wind on your skin
MEDITATE	Fix your thoughts on something (person/place/thing) that makes you happy
PRAY	Say a prayer that helps calm and re-center you
LISTEN	Play uplifting music/podcast/TED Talk
CONNECT	Call a friend who is a good listener or one who makes you laugh
PET	Spend time with a friendly pet
DRINK	Enjoy some warm calming tea
WALK	Take a 10-minute walk outdoors
RECITE	Tell yourself positive affirmations
ASK	Request a hug or support from a loved one
WATCH	Get lost in a funny movie
REST	Take a nap or lay down … be still
COLOR	Doodle, paint, or print free adult coloring books
COZY UP	Wrap yourself up in a warm blanket or throw on a comfy robe
EAT	Treat yourself to your favorite meal/dessert/snack
DATE	Take yourself or your partner on an impromptu date
DRESS UP	Get dressed up for no reason at all
REMINISCE	Visit or think of child memories that bring you joy
READ	Read inspirational/uplifting quotes

SELF-CARE

Self-care is the intentional practice to increase activities that promote wellness into your daily and or weekly routine. There are different categories of self-care, including: physical, emotional, psychological/intellectual, social, and spiritual.

Key: Think More Prevention vs. Intervention

ACTIVITIES

- ⭕ Commit to yoga
- ⭕ Increase nature walks
- ⭕ Regular movement (i.e., Stretches, exercise, bike rides, etc.)
- ⭕ Journaling
- ⭕ Volunteering
- ⭕ Social media breaks (as needed or scheduled)
- ⭕ Read a new book
- ⭕ Daily or weekly bubble baths
- ⭕ Initiate a night out with friends and/or partner
- ⭕ Increase rest (i.e., Nap, go to bed earlier)
- ⭕ Regularly put phone on 'do not disturb'
- ⭕ Create a vision board
- ⭕ Learn a new language
- ⭕ Name 2 things you are grateful for

- ⭕ Gardening
- ⭕ Pamper yourself frequently (mani/pedi, haircut, massage, etc)
- ⭕ Tap into your creativity (paint, write, bake, Sew, etc.)
- ⭕ Enroll in a dance class
- ⭕ Create an uplifting music playlist
- ⭕ Incorporate candles and soothing music during your shower/bath time routine
- ⭕ Participate in meditation/prayer daily or weekly
- ⭕ Create a morning or evening routine
- ⭕ Create and frequently reference an Affirmations list
- ⭕ De-clutter often and donate items that you no longer use
- ⭕ Create healthier boundaries with friends and family… and stick with the boundaries
- ⭕ Take the 'scenic route' home from time to time
- ⭕ Take yourself out on a weekly/monthly solo date (movies, coffee, dessert, etc.)

*Self-care activities and coping skills are interrelated. Coping skills can become a part of your self-care routine when practiced more habitually. And self-care activites can be used as coping skills when applied in the moment of discomfort with the intention of regulating your current emotions. The key point is to create a self-care routine, which will help you recognize and manage emotional discomfort more efficiently.

STAGES OF GRIEF

The stages of infertility grief are not linear and some would argue that there are more than 5 stages. However, in this journal, we will be referencing the Kübler-Ross Model. Use the diagram below to help you identify the stages of grief and the thoughts and feelings you are experiencing.

GRIEF

DENIAL
Ex: This isn't really happening to us... It can't be!

ANGER
Ex: I hate this! How is everyone pregnant but me? Even people who don't want to be pregnant are pregnant. This has to be a cruel joke.

BARGAINING
Ex: Maybe if I pray harder it'll happen. Maybe if I never got that abortion...

DEPRESSION
Ex: I feel hopeless. It's never going to happen for me. I feel so sad. I don't want to hear about anymore baby announcements.

ACCEPTANCE
Ex: This is our journey...It's not what I wanted, but it's ours. I feel optimistic. This is rough, but I feel hopeful after meeting with the doctor.

COGNITIVE WHEEL

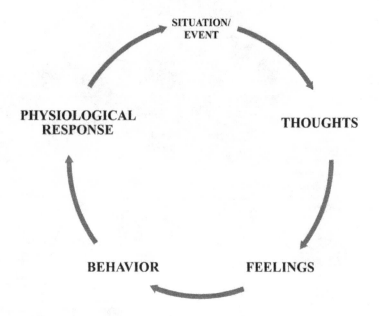

SITUATION/
EVENT

THOUGHTS

PHYSIOLOGICAL
RESPONSE

BEHAVIOR

FEELINGS

Carve out time to
reflect, process,
and reconnect
with YOU!

Carve out time to
reflect, process,
and reconnect
with YOU!

Carve out time to
reflect, process,
and reconnect
with YOU!

Carve out time to
reflect, process,
and reconnect
with YOU!

Carve out time to
reflect, process,
and reconnect
with YOU!

MY BABY JOURNEY

Carve out time to
reflect, process,
and reconnect
with YOU!

92

Carve out time to
reflect, process,
and reconnect
with YOU!

Carve out time to
reflect, process,
and reconnect
with YOU!

MY BABY JOURNEY

Carve out time to
reflect, process,
and reconnect
with YOU!

95

Carve out time to
reflect, process,
and reconnect
with YOU!

DATE / /

Carve out time to reflect, process, and reconnect with YOU!

DATE / /

Carve out time to
reflect, process,
and reconnect
with YOU!

DATE / /

Carve out time to reflect, process, and reconnect with YOU!

MY BABY JOURNEY

DATE / /

MY BABY JOURNEY

105

Carve out time to
reflect, process,
and reconnect
with YOU!

106

Carve out time to
reflect, process,
and reconnect
with YOU!

112

Carve out time to
reflect, process,
and reconnect
with YOU!

Carve out time to
reflect, process,
and reconnect
with YOU!

114

Carve out time to
reflect, process,
and reconnect
with YOU!

Carve out time to
reflect, process,
and reconnect
with YOU!

Carve out time to
reflect, process,
and reconnect
with YOU!

MY BABY JOURNEY

Carve out time to
reflect, process,
and reconnect
with YOU!

Carve out time to
reflect, process,
and reconnect
with YOU!

124

Carve out time to
reflect process,
and reconnect
with YOU!

Carve out time to
reflect, process,
and reconnect
with YOU!

126

Carve out time to
reflect. process,
and reconnect
with YOU!

132

Carve out time to
reflect, process,
and reconnect
with YOU!

Carve out time to
reflect, process,
and reconnect
with YOU!

134

Carve out time to
reflect, process,
and reconnect
with YOU!

135

Carve out time to
reflect, process,
and reconnect
with YOU!

References

Centers for Disease Control and Prevention. (2021, April 13). Division of Reproductive Health. Retrieved from https://www.cdc.gov/reproductivehealth/infertility/index.htm

Gnoth C, Godehardt D, Godehardt E, Frank-Herrmann P, Freundl G. Time to pregnancy: Results of the German prospective study and impact on the management of infertility. *Hum Reprod.* 2003;18(9):1959-66. doi:10.1093/humrep/deg366

Rooney K & Domar A. The relationship between stress and infertility. *Dialogues in Clinical Neuroscience.* 2018 Mar; 20(1): 40-47.

Wenzel, Amy, Coping with Infertility, Miscarriage, and Neonatal Loss (2014).

Wenzel, Amy and Kleiman, Karen, Cognitive Behavioral Therapy for Perinatal Distress (2014).

Resources

https://www.karenthetherapist.com

https://www.postpartum.net/get-help/

https://www.fertilityforcoloredgirls.org/

https://thebrokenbrownegg.org/

https://www.bornintosilence.org/

https://resolve.org/

https://pved.org/

https://www.singlemothersbychoice.org/

https://undefiningmotherhood.com/

https://www.inciid.org/

http://www.choicemoms.org/

https://fertility.rescripted.com/

https://www.fertilityhelphub.com/

https://www.fertilityoutloud.com/

https://www.fertilityiq.com/

https://www.throughtheheart.org/

https://infertilityawareness.org/

https://www.maternalmentalhealthnow.org/

https://blackmamasmatter.org/